SA

TRONG MAN'S STRENGTH

TOLD BY CARINE MACKENZIE
ILLUSTRATIONS BY FRED APPS

10 9 8 7 6 5 4 3 2 1

Published by Christian Focus Publications, Geanies House,
Fearn, Tain, Ross-shire, IV20 1TW, Scotland, U.K.
Printed in China.
ISBN: 978-1-78191-328-4
www.christianfocus.com

CF4•K

God's people, the Israelites, turned their back on God and continually sinned. God was displeased and punished them by allowing their enemies, the Philistines, to rule over them for forty years. But God had a plan to save them.

Among the Israelites was a good man called Manoah. One day an angel of the Lord appeared to Manoah's wife. He told her that she would have a baby boy, who would save God's people from their enemies, the Philistines.

Manoah prayed that God would teach them how to bring up their son. The angel came again and gave them special instructions. The boy was to be a Nazirite, not to take wine or strong drink, nor to cut his hair.

Manoah offered to make some food for God's messenger, but he declined. 'Offer a burnt offering to God instead,' he suggested.

When Manoah's wife had a baby boy, they called him Samson. As he grew up, the Lord blessed him and prepared him for God's work.

Samson grew up to be a strong young man. He remembered his Nazirite vow and never cut his hair. One day he went to Timnah and noticed a young Philistine woman. He came home to his parents and asked them to arrange a marriage. His parents would have preferred an Israelite girl, but Samson insisted, 'She is the right one for me.'

This was all part of God's plan for Samson to fight against the Philistines, the oppressors of God's people. Samson and his parents made the journey to Timnah. On the way a young lion roared up towards them. The Spirit of the Lord rushed on Samson and he received extra strength. He was able to tear the lion to pieces with his bare hands.

The marriage was arranged. Some days later Samson went back to Timnah for the wedding. He went to look at the carcase of the lion he had killed. In it was a swarm of bees and honey. Samson scraped out some honey and gave some to his parents too, but he did not tell them where he got it from.

Thirty young men attended Samson's wedding to the Philistine girl in Timnah.

'I will give you a riddle,' said Samson. 'If you can solve it, I will give you each a linen garment and a change of clothing. If not, you must give me thirty sets of clothes. Here is the riddle.

Out of the eater came something to eat.

Out of the strong came something sweet.'

For three days they puzzled but could not solve the riddle. On the fourth day they tackled Samson's bride. They threatened to burn down her father's house if she did not manage to get Samson to tell her the answer.

'You don't love me,' Samson's wife wept to him.

'I have not told anyone, not even my parents,' replied Samson. For the seven days of the feast, she wept and nagged. At last Samson gave in and told her. She immediately told the young men at the wedding.

The men came up to Samson with the solution.

‘What’s sweeter than honey? What is stronger than a lion?’

Samson immediately realised that his wife had betrayed him and told his secret.

The Spirit of the Lord came upon him and strengthened him. Samson went to Ashkelon, killed thirty men and took their clothes. He gave the set of clothes as the prize to the thirty young men as he had promised.

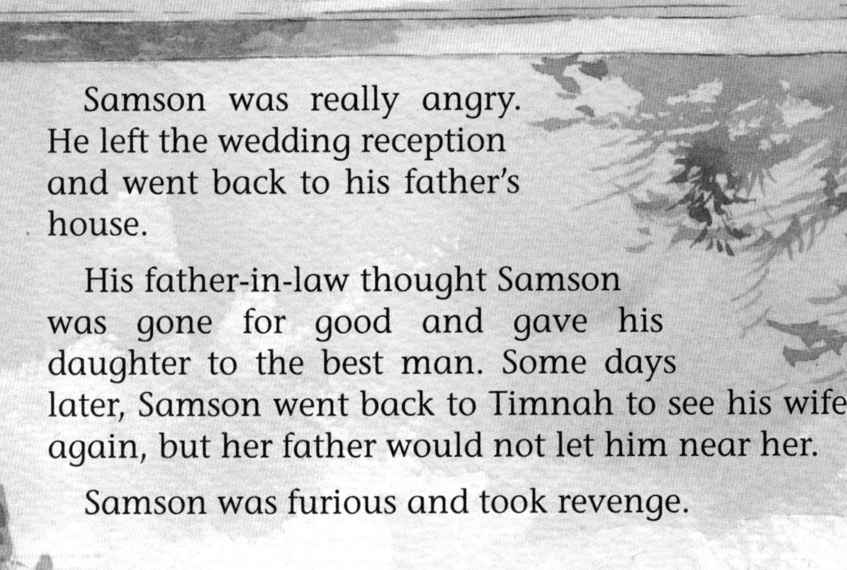

Samson was really angry. He left the wedding reception and went back to his father's house.

His father-in-law thought Samson was gone for good and gave his daughter to the best man. Some days later, Samson went back to Timnah to see his wife again, but her father would not let him near her.

Samson was furious and took revenge.

Samson caught 300 foxes, tied them in pairs by the tail and put a torch between the tails. He set fire to the torches and let the foxes go into the standing grain belonging to the Philistines. The grain and the olive orchards went up in flames. When the Philistines heard the reason for Samson's anger, they took revenge on his wife and father-in-law. Samson attacked the Philistines again furiously and then went to live in a cave at Etam.

The Philistines attacked the land of Judah, wanting to capture Samson.

Three thousand men of Judah came to get Samson at the cave. 'What have you done? Don't you know that the Philistines are our rulers?' they asked.

'I only paid them back,' argued Samson.

'We have come to capture you and take you to the Philistines,' they replied.

So they tied him up with two ropes and took him from the cave.

When they reached Lehi, the Philistines rushed towards him shouting.

The Spirit of the Lord again gave Samson special strength. The ropes binding him were snapped like threads.

Samson grabbed the jawbone of a donkey, and killed 1,000 men.

Samson was very thirsty. He called out to God, 'You have granted this great salvation by the hand of your servant; must I now die of thirst?'

God caused water to gush from a hollow in the ground and the drink revived Samson. God graciously heard his prayer.

For the next twenty years, Samson was the leader of God's people in Israel.

Samson fell in love with a woman called Delilah. The Philistine leaders came to her and demanded that she find out what made Samson so strong. They wanted to overpower him and put him in chains. 'We will each give you 1,100 pieces of silver,' they promised.

Delilah begged Samson to tell her his secret. 'How could someone overpower you?'

'If they tied me up with seven fresh bow strings, I would be as weak as anyone,' replied Samson.

When she got the chance, Delilah did that. 'The Philistines are here!' she called. Samson snapped the bow strings like thread.

He had not revealed the secret of his strength.

'You have mocked me and told lies,' Delilah complained. 'Please tell me how you could be bound.'

Samson gave another answer. 'If they bind me with new ropes then I shall be as weak as any other man.' But again when the Philistines burst into the room, Samson snapped the ropes easily.

'You have mocked me and told me lies,' Delilah whined again. 'Tell me how you can be tied up?'

'If you were to weave seven locks of my hair into a loom and fasten it tight, then I would be as weak as any other man,' Samson replied.

So Delilah did that while he slept.

'The Philistines are here, Samson!' she called.

Samson woke up and with one jerk had freed himself from the loom.

Samson's secret was still safe.

'How can you say you love me when you don't confide in me?' Delilah wheedled. 'You have mocked me three times and told me lies.'

Day after day she nagged him, until he couldn't stand it any longer.

'My hair has never been cut. I have been a Nazirite to God since birth,' Samson confessed. 'If my head is shaved, my strength will leave me.'

Samson had at last told the truth and Delilah realised it. She lulled him to sleep with his head in her lap, then brought a barber to shave his head. As she tormented him, she could see that his strength was gone.

When Samson awoke he thought he would be as strong as ever. But sadly, the Lord had left him. His strength was gone and the Philistines were able to capture him.

The Philistine enemy gouged out his eyes and blind, weak Samson was taken to Gaza and chained with bronze shackles. He was forced to grind grain at the millstone in the prison. During this time of hard forced labour, Samson's hair began to grow again.

The Philistines were elated that Samson was now their prisoner. They held a party where they made sacrifices to the false god, Dagon.

'Bring out Samson to entertain us,' they shouted gleefully. The house was full of men and women, about 3,000 on the balcony.

Samson was made to stand between two pillars in the grand building. The Philistines gloated over his condition.

'Let me feel the pillars,' Samson said to the young man leading him.

Samson called out to God in prayer, 'O Lord God remember me. Please strengthen me just this once more, so that I would be avenged for my two eyes.'

Samson grasped the two pillars and leant his weight on them – to the right and to the left.

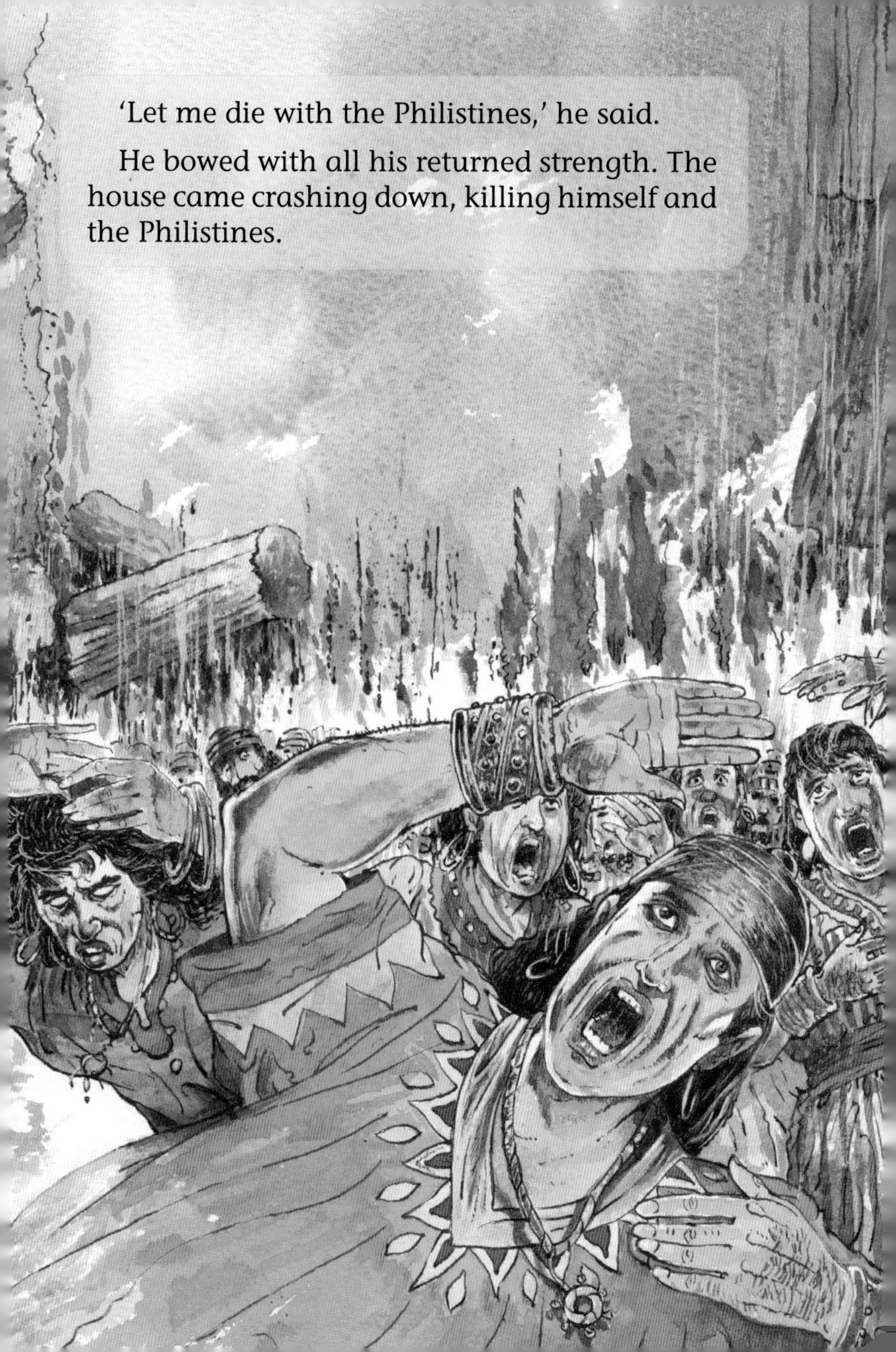

'Let me die with the Philistines,' he said.

He bowed with all his returned strength. The house came crashing down, killing himself and the Philistines.

When the temple fell down it not only crushed the people who were in it but it came down on top of all the Philistine rulers. Samson killed more at his death than he had in his lifetime. His relatives came to Gaza and took his body back home to be buried beside his father.

Samson had many faults and failures, yet God used him to fight against the enemy of his people. He was described even before he was born as 'the one who would begin to save Israel'. Even as a sinful, imperfect man, God used him in the fight against the oppressor.

God has provided us with a perfect Saviour, the Lord Jesus Christ, who will conquer all his and our enemies. Jesus is sinless and lived a perfect life on this earth. We read in the book of Hebrews that Jesus Christ understands what it is like to be tempted yet he is without sin. God used Samson to save Israel – but he wasn't perfect, he was a sinner. God's perfect plan for salvation was to send his Son, Jesus Christ, to save sinners – from every tribe, nation and language.

Samson was a judge and was God's chosen man to rescue the people of Israel from their enemies. Jesus died on the cross to save his people from the enemy of sin. He has fully accomplished this great salvation. One day he will return as is promised in the Scripture and he will judge the whole world.